A CURRICULUM WORKBOOK

THE REBIRTH OF MUSIC WORKBOOK

DISCOVER THE MEANING AND PURPOSE OF MUSIC

LAMAR BOSCHMAN

THE REBIRTH OF MUSIC WORKBOOK
Copyright 2017 by LaMar Boschman All rights reserved
Printed in the United States of America

ISBN (print): 978-0998054537

This book or parts thereof may not be reproduced in any form without prior written permission of the publisher.

Unless otherwise noted, all Scripture quotations are from the New King James Version of the Bible. Copyright © 1979, 1980, 1982 by Thomas Nelson Inc. publishers. Used by permission.

Scripture quotations marked AMP are from the Amplified Bible. Old Testament copyright © 1965, 1987 by the Zondervan Corporation.

The Amplified New Testament copyright © 1954, 1958, 1987 by the Lockman Foundation. Used by permission.

Scripture quotations marked KJV are from the King James Version of the Bible.

Scripture quotations marked NAS are from the New American Standard Bible. Copyright © 1960, 1962, 1963, 1968, 1971, 1972, 1973, 1975, 1977 by the Lockman Foundation. Used by permission.

Scripture quotations marked NEB are from the New English Bible. Copyright © 1961, 1970 by the Delegates of the Oxford University Press and the Syndics of the Cambridge University Press. Used by permission.

Scripture quotations marked NIV are from the Holy Bible, New International Version. Copyright © 1973, 1978, 1984, International Bible Society. Used by permission.

Scripture quotations marked RSV are from the Revised Standard Version of the Bible. Copyright © 1946, 1952, 1971 by the Division of Christian Education of the National Council of the Churches of Christ in the USA. Used by permission.

Cover Design - Kylie Rott
Proofing Editor - Katherine Harrold

LAMARBOSCHMAN.COM

TABLE OF CONTENTS

v   **PREFACE**

7   LESSON ONE
MUSIC, ANGELS AND LUCIFER

19   LESSON TWO
MUSIC AND SATAN

31   LESSON THREE
MUSIC AND ITS IMPORTANCE

43   LESSON FOUR
MUSIC AND THE PRESENCE OF GOD

53   LESSON FIVE
MUSIC AND THE PROPHETIC

65   LESSON SIX
MUSIC IN WAR

75   LESSON SEVEN
MUSIC AND HEALING

89   LESSON EIGHT
MUSIC AND EXORCISM

99   LESSON NINE
WHICH MUSIC IS OK?

111	**LESSON TEN** **MUSIC, RESTORATION AND REVIVAL**
121	**LESSON ELEVEN** **MUSIC IN HEAVEN**
131	**LESSON TWELVE** **MUSIC AND PRAISE**

141	**ABOUT THE AUTHOR**

PREFACE

Theology is the study of God. Some consider it boring and heady - stuffy thinking for professors and theologians. However, they can not be more wrong. Theology is for everyone and critical to everyone.

Webster dictionary defines theology as "the science of God; the sciences of the existence, character, and attributes of God, his laws and government, the doctrines we are to believe, and the duties we are to practice. . . the science of Christian faith and life." A simple definition of what Webster wrote is the study of religious faith, practice, and experience: the study of God and God's relationship to the world.

Everything is affected by your theology. Theology itself provides a foundation for your philosophy and worldview, which in turn sets inclinations for your heart, actions, and decisions in all situations. In short, theology is a set of intellectual and emotional commitments about God and man which dictate ones beliefs and actions. Theology is relevant to all, as well as, the concepts which it seeks to articulate. It is pimarily the pursuit of the knowledge of God and His perspective on all things.

Have you ever wondered what God's view is of music? It will form and forge your outlook of music in both the secular and sacred realms.

During this study you will discover the Biblical truths about music in God's kingdom. In other words you will discover the theology of music. This theology will help you discern the music of God's kingdom and be empowered as a spiritual music maker. Without the correct theology of music you will be unaware of God's purpose for music, misuse it, fall short of its purpose, and make yourself vulnerable to evil plots of dark forces.

I pray you will feel excitement and intrigue in this exploration of music of the kingdom of God, as well as be empowered to be a Biblical music maker.

—LAMAR BOSCHMAN

1

LESSON ONE
MUSIC, ANGELS, AND LUCIFER

"Aside from the redeemed, angels are perhaps the most musically active worshipers in heaven."

– LaMar Boschman

LESSON ONE - MUSIC, ANGELS AND LUCIFER
STUDY GUIDE

ARCHANGELS

1. List the three archangels mentioned in Jude 1:9, Luke 1:19 and Isaiah 14:12.

_____
_____
_____
_____

2. What was the name and purpose of the archangel who fought Satan and the Prince of Persia? (Daniel 10:13, 21; Rev 12:7)

_____
_____
_____
_____
_____

3. What was the name and purpose of the archangel who told Mary she would give birth to Jesus? (Luke 1:26)

_____
_____
_____
_____

4. Long before God made men and formed the earth, as we know it today, He created an angel and gave him the ability to play music. What was his name and purpose? (Isa 14:11; Ezek 28:14)

_____
_____
_____
_____
_____

THE MUSIC ANGEL

5. One archangel could play music. What musical instruments did he have? (Ezek 28:13; Isa 14:11 Read NKJV)

_____
_____
_____
_____

6. God created the angels to worship Him. What was Lucifer's possible role in worship?

_____
_____
_____
_____
_____

7. What could this archangel play with these instruments – rhythm, chords or melody; or all three? Explain why.

_____
_____
_____
_____
_____

8. What three attributes of Lucifer are mentioned in Ezekiel 28:17?

_____
_____
_____
_____
_____
_____
_____
_____

9. Music in the kingdom of heaven was created for one purpose. What was it? (Ezek 28:13,14)
_____
_____
_____
_____

THE FALL OF THE MUSIC ANGEL

10. Everything about Lucifer was perfect from the day he was created. But then, in the midst of all the harmony, order and divine music in heaven, what did he begin to desire for himself? (Isa 14:13-14)
_____
_____
_____
_____

11. Describe what happened to Lucifer in Ezekiel 28:16-17 and Isaiah 14:12 after he declared his ambitious desires exposing his motives.
_____
_____
_____
_____

12. As a result of Lucifer's attitude and actions, war broke out in heaven. Describe what happened. (Rev 12:3,7-9)

_____
_____
_____
_____

13. What does God think of pride? Include James 4:6 and Proverbs 16:18 in your answer.

_____
_____
_____
_____
_____
_____
_____

14. Did God take away Lucifer's ability to play music when He cast him to the earth? (Ezek 28:13-19)

_____
_____
_____

MUSIC OF THE GODS

15. When did music leave the realm of God's kingdom and go secular? (Isaiah 14:1)

_____
_____
_____
_____

16. The Bible says that worms surround Lucifer and his music. What kind were they and what do they do? (Isaiah 14:11)

_____
_____
_____
_____

17. In your own words, what does Lucifer's attitude and ambition say to you?

_____
_____
_____
_____
_____

IN ADDITION

ANGELS & MUSIC

The record of Job's conversation with God is one of the few accounts in divine writings that give us a clue to the role of music in the beginning of time. God revealed to Job that music was present at the creation of the earth. God gave Job insight into the role that music played before man or the earth was born. Describing the earth God said...

> On what were its footings set, or who laid its cornerstone—while the morning stars sang together and all the angels shouted for joy?
>
> Job 38:6-7 (NIV)

FIRST SINGERS

Music is older than man and predates the earth itself. Before there was a ball called earth with land and sea, there was music. As long as there were angels there was music. These star-angels were among the first luminaries. Before the dawn of time they shone brightly. God commanded their light to shine out of darkness upon this lower world, the arena where heaven and earth was formless and void.

These "morning stars" or "sons of God" refer to intelligent beings that existed before the creation of the visible heavens and earth. Some interpreters of scripture suggest that they are the same type of angel. These angels were among the first in the order of creation but possibly not the highest in rank.

Can you imagine what it must have sounded like when God said, "Let there be light!" and the angels sang in a jubilant response to the creative work of Jesus?

They lifted up their voices in exaltation crying out in spontaneous songs of praise at the glorious display of Jesus's miraculous power. What a celestial musical! Perhaps it was because the angels were so overwhelmed by the powerful and perfect display of creative power that they burst into joyful song.

MORNING STARS

The Hebrew word for "morning" is "dawn" meaning "break of day" or "early." Since these angels were among the first creatures to be created, they were the "early" stars. They were present at the dawn of creation.

Scholars call these angelic beings, of the morning of time, "dawn angels." These beautiful stars are said to sing God's praises.

> Praise Him you shining stars!
>
> Psalms 148:3b

Other writers say these morning stars were armies of angels who sang and shouted for joy, when they saw earth's foundations laid. Although the earth was not made for them, yet they knew that the eternal Word would cause the earth, out of all the trillions of galaxies, to be the single habitation and focus of God's love and affection.

The word for "sang" is to "creak, to shout aloud for joy, cry out, greatly rejoice, cause to sing aloud, to sing for joy, triumph." In other words the song of this angel choir was boisterous, noisy, and very emotional. They did not rejoice with average joy but with great jubilation.

The word for "shouted" is "to split the ears with sound, to shout (for alarm or joy), blow or sound an alarm, cry (alarm, aloud), destroy, make a joyful noise." Wow! These masses of celestial luminaries made a such a joyful shout that it sharply penetrated the expanse of the heavens. I wonder what the song was like! What tones or frequencies they made. I wonder, "What did they sing? What did they shout?"

DISCUSSION

18. Was there music before the earth and man was created? If so, who made the music?

_____
_____
_____
_____

19. Describe the music that predates the creation of the earth.

_____
_____
_____
_____
_____
_____

20. Describe the first singers recorded in the Bible.

_____
_____
_____
_____
_____
_____
_____
_____
_____
_____
_____
_____

2

LESSON TWO
MUSIC AND SATAN

"I deliberately present myself as a personification of the devil."
- Mick Jagger

LESSON TWO - MUSIC AND SATAN
STUDY GUIDE

> For you said to yourself, "I will ascend to heaven and rule the angels. I will take the highest throne. I will preside on the Mount of Assembly far away in the north. I will climb to the highest heavens and be like the Most High."
> Isaiah 14:13-14 (TLB)

LUCIFER'S LUST

1. What does Satan, previously called Lucifer, want from Jesus in Matthew 4:8-11?

_____
_____
_____
_____
_____
_____
_____

2. What did Jesus do in response to Satan's temptation? (Matt 4:10)
_____
_____
_____
_____
_____

3. What should your response be when tempted with pride?
_____
_____
_____
_____
_____

MUSIC OF SATAN

4. How are non-Christian musicians different than Christian musicians?
_____
_____
_____
_____
_____
_____

5. What is Lucifer offering musicians today?

6. Name four artists or music groups that you think represent or personify evil.

7. If some secular music can be evil how is it harmful to the listener or fan? Explain.

8. How is Satan working behind the scenes in musicians and their music?
___
___
___
___
___

9. What is Satan trying to accomplish through the music that has his nature?
___
___
___
___
___

SATANIC STRATEGY

10. In John 8:44, Jesus told the Pharisees their father was the devil because they acted like him. How does that relate to musicians who act like Satan?
___
___
___
___
___

11. Who are the children of the Devil and how do we know?

_____
_____
_____
_____
_____

12. When you lie, how are you acting like Satan - the Father of Lies?

_____
_____
_____
_____
_____

13. When you lie, or deceive others, in that moment how are you coming under the power of the Father of Lies - the Deceiver?

_____
_____
_____
_____
_____

14. What did Trent Reznor of Nine Inch Nails promote in one of his songs?

_____
_____
_____
_____
_____

15. How is music a doorway to the spirit world?

_____
_____
_____
_____
_____

HIS SATANIC MAJESTY'S REQUEST

16. How does music put thoughts of suicide, sex and murder into the listener's mind, and how would that aid Satan's work in the earth?

_____
_____
_____
_____

17. What active force makes evil alluring to people?

18. How does sex and darkness help make groups popular and their music more desirable?

19. Why do depraved musicians perform sinful or dark acts on stage?

20. What does Romans 12:1 say we should do with our bodies?

_____
_____
_____
_____
_____

21. Jim Morrison, of the rock band Doors, was arrested for doing sexual acts on stage where the average age of the audience was 12-14. He said, "When I'm performing I'm spiritual!" What kind of fruit did Morrison's actions impart into the lives and spirits of the pre-teens present?

_____
_____
_____
_____
_____

TRUE WORSHIP VERSUS DISHONEST WORSHIP

22. The Bible says in John 4:24 that God is searching for spirit and truth worshipers. What kind of worshipers is Satan looking for?

_____
_____
_____
_____

23. God's Word is truth. How will knowing God's Word help you discern the works and plots of your enemy?

_____
_____
_____
_____

IN ADDITION

WORSHIP OF DEMONS

Animism is the worship of evil spirits. Sometimes music is used as an "expression of demons" or it is used to express "worship of demons." A century ago, only anthropologist and missionaries talked about animism. But with the revival of spirit-ism, coupled with the migration of numerous animistic peoples to North America, animism is growing in popularity.

POP CULTURE ZOMBIES

Today pop culture is enamored with demons, vampires, zombies, ghosts and witches. Media companies, from Disney to Twentieth Century Fox, wanting to follow the trends of the culture unknowingly promote the work of

Satan. The presence of paranormal or supernaturally dark themes has increased more than 500% according to one survey. In fact, it is the theme of more than 30% of all movies, games and TV shows.

When people go see movies or role-playing games that portray the paranormal, they open themselves up to be abused by the kingdom of darkness. They are stimulated to think evil thoughts and feel evil feelings—all in the name of entertainment. People leave the game or the theatre numb and dumb to the Satanic work they were just immersed in. If the impact is strong enough people walk around dazed—as if under a spell.

Judson Cornwall, a pioneer of the theology of worship, wrote "Satan is still far more interested in worship than in sin. He is most likely to be in the church than in the worst den of iniquity in any area. This fallen angel would rather pervert a person's worship than corrupt his morals, for he knows that if he can pervert our worship, we will corrupt our morals."[1]

Our theology of worship is absolutely essential to live and worship God correctly. But also to not be deceived by spirits of darkness or the world that would cuorrupt us morally and destroy our lives.

---

1   Cornwall, Judson *Whose War is It Anyway?* pg 29

DISCUSSION

24. How is exposure to darkness through movies, TV shows, and games one of the covert military strategies Satan uses to destroy us?

_____
_____
_____
_____

25. Why would Satan be more interested in perverting our worship than promoting sin?

_____
_____
_____
_____
_____
_____
_____
_____
_____

3

LESSON THREE
MUSIC AND ITS IMPORTANCE

"Music is the language of God. We musicians are as close to God as man can be. We hear his voice, we read His lips, we give birth to the children of God, who sing His praise. That's what musicians are."

– Ludwig van Beetheoven

LESSON THREE - MUSIC AND ITS IMPORTANCE
STUDY GUIDE

MUSIC AND THE PRESENCE OF GOD

1. Music must be important to God because it is mentioned in the Bible often. Approximately how many times is music mentioned in scripture?

_____
_____
_____
_____
_____

2. Psalms 100:2 gives a protocol for coming before God, the Holy One. What is that protocol?

_____
_____
_____
_____
_____

MUSIC AND ITS IMPORTANCE 33

3. What does Psalm 95:2 in the NIV say to you?
_____
_____
_____
_____
_____

4. Write out two Bible verses that talk about music.
_____
_____
_____
_____
_____

5. Psalms 22:3 says, "You are Holy enthroned on the praises of Israel." What does the later part of that verse mean?
_____
_____
_____
_____

6. What is the Hebrew word of "praise" in Psalm 22:3 and what does it mean?
_____
_____
_____
_____
_____

MUSICIANS WANTED

King David receivied the greatest revelation of the importance and relevance of music in all of scriptures. So much so that he appointed Levites as singers and musicians to minister in music before the presence of God continually.

> And these are they whom David set over the service of song in the house of the Lord, after that the ark had rest. And they ministered before the dwelling place of the tabernacle of the congregation with singing, until Solomon had built the house of the Lord in Jerusalem: and then they waited [served] on their office according to their [assigned] order.
>
> 1 Chronicles 6:31-32

7. Why do you think David appointed singers to sing in the tabernacle?

_____
_____
_____
_____

8. How were the musicians and singers supported financially?

_____
_____
_____

9. In 1 Chronicles 9:33 it says the singers were free from other responsibilities so they could do something that was of most importance to King David. What was that?

_____
_____
_____
_____
_____

10. What does Nehemiah 11:22-23 say about the Levitical singers?

_____
_____
_____
_____
_____

11. Based on the scriptures you've read, how important would you say the ministry of singing is to God?

_____
_____
_____
_____
_____
_____

ROLE OF MUSIC IN PUBLIC WORSHIP

12. What do some people consider the musical part of the service to be?

_____
_____
_____
_____
_____

13. What effect does musical praise and worship have on us?

_____
_____
_____
_____
_____

14. In 2 Kings 3 Elisha the prophet, who could hear and speak for God, needed a musician to do so. In your own words explain why.

_____
_____
_____
_____
_____

15. What happened when the musician played in 2 Kings 3:15?

_____
_____
_____
_____
_____

SINGING - PART OF OUR DAILY WORSHIP

16. What does Psalm 96:1 tell us about why music is important?

_____
_____
_____
_____
_____

17. In The Rebirth of Music textbook how many times does it say we are instructed to sing in the Bible?

_____
_____
_____
_____
_____

THE STRENGTH OF PRAISE AND WORSHIP

18. In the textbook, it is mentioned that musical praise and worship is crucial and relevant more than ever before. Why is that?

_____
_____
_____
_____

19. The longest book in the Bible is a songbook of prayers and praise to God. How does that show us the importance of music to God?

_____
_____
_____
_____
_____
_____

GOD SINGS

The Bible says in Zephaniah 3:17 that God sings. "The Lord your God in your midst, the Mighty One, will save; He will rejoice over you with gladness, He will quiet you with His love, He will rejoice over you with singing."

20. In your opinion, in Zephaniah 3:17, is it a metaphor or does God actually rejoice over you with singing?
_____
_____
_____
_____
_____

21. How does God singing make singing important to us?
_____
_____
_____
_____
_____

22. What does it say in Hebrews 2:12 about the music Jesus makes?
_____
_____
_____
_____
_____
_____
_____
_____
_____

23. Where does Hebrews 2 tell us Jesus is when He sings?
_____
_____
_____
_____
_____

24. What scripture tells us that the Holy Spirit sings?
_____
_____
_____
_____
_____

IN ADDITION

MUSIC'S IMPORTANCE

In the awakening that came under Hezekiah's leadership, one of the first things to be restored was the song of the Lord and the anointing on the music. During that time Hezekiah appointed the singers and the musicians just as Nehemiah did:

> And he [Hezekiah] set the Levites in the house of the Lord with CYMBALS, with

> PSALTERIES, and with HARPS, according to the commandment of David, and of Gad the king's seer, and Nathan the prophet: for so was the commandment of the Lord by his prophets.
>
> 2 Chronicles 29:25 (Emphasis mine)

This verse clearly points out that God has commanded, through His prophets, that music is a ministry that should be set up according to His pattern, which is found in the tabernacle of David.

> The Levites stood with the INSTRUMENTS of David, and the priests with the TRUMPETS. And Hezekiah commanded to offer the burnt offering upon the altar. And when the burnt offering began, the SONG OF THE LORD began also with the TRUMPETS, and with the INSTRUMENTS ordained by David king of Israel. And all the congregation worshipped, and the SINGERS SANG, and the TRUMPETERS SOUNDED.
>
> 2 Chronicles 29:26-28a (Emphasis mine)

Hezekiah, like David, had a heart for worship. He knew the law of Moses and the commandments of David and the prophecies of Nathan. He knew how to set God's house in order. That is what is called Revival.

Music is an evidence of a rebirth in God's people. When they receive again a revelation of truth, they will experience again a joyous sound. You show me a church that loves to sing and I'll show you a church that is spiritually alive. You show me a person that can't find it within himself to sing and rejoice, and I'll show you someone who has nothing to sing about. You show me a musician that is bubbling over with joyful music and I'll show you a musician who has a fresh revelation of Jesus.

DISCUSSION

25. Describe two things about music in 2 Chronicles 29:26-28 that strike you.

_____
_____
_____
_____
_____
_____
_____
_____
_____
_____

4

LESSON FOUR
MUSIC AND THE PRESENCE OF GOD

"Where there is devotional music, God is always at hand with His gracious presence."

– Johannes Sebastian Bach

LESSON FOUR - MUSIC & THE PRESENCE OF GOD
STUDY GUIDE

Music in the kingdom of God is spiritual and goes beyond the realm of creating art. Supernatural music making involves the musician's heart, Biblical principles, and the Holy Spirit.

KINGDOM MUSICIANS

1. What did God mean when He said in Numbers 8:14 "the Levites will be Mine?"

___
___
___
___
___
___
___
___
___

2. Some of the Levites were porters of the Ark of the Covenant. What other responsibilities did the Levites have? (1 Chronicles 9:33)

___

3. What does 1 Chronicles 15:16 say that King David did regarding music?

___

4. What age were the Levites and how many of them were in David's ministry?

___

5. David had a very large worship department in Jerusalem. How many of the Levites were players of musical instruments?

_____
_____
_____
_____

MUSICIANS OF THE PRESENCE

6. Where was the presence of God in David's day?

_____
_____
_____
_____

7. It was the responsibility of the singing Levites to carry the Ark of the Covenant. What does that mean to you today?

_____
_____
_____
_____

8. Later in Solomon's temple music was connected with God's manifest presence. What happened in 2 Chronicles 5:13-14?

9. What Biblical principles were enacted when the musicians played and God's revealed presence came in power?

10. How do you become a musician who has the power and presence of God in your music?

FOR HIS EYES ONLY

11. For whose pleasure is worship music played and sung? Why?

_____
_____
_____
_____

12. For two thousand years the Bride of Christ has gathered to worship her Groom. How important is it that there is a flow in worship and that the service is not chopped up into parts?

_____
_____
_____
_____

13. What are some things leaders, including the worship leader, can do to facilitate the people connecting better with the presence of God?

_____
_____
_____
_____

IN ADDITION

PRESENCE OF THE KINGDOM

Dr. Jack Hayford said, "Worship has often been misunderstood as the musical prelude to the sermon, rather than the means by which we, as the people of God, invite the dominion of His Kingdom to be established on earth."

The rule and reign of God is experienced in the place where we invite His reign and are submitted to His rule. His dominion does not just happen everywhere. There are those who refuse God's rule, disregard His wishes and disobey His commands. Those choices put people under the authority of the prince of the power of the air...the dominion of Satan.

God's presence and dominion is revealed and evident when we sing "tehillah" praise to God. Though He is everywhere He is not evident everywhere. However, in the melodic praise of His people the Bible says He sits and rules. There the dominon of His kingdom is present in power.

MUSIC IN SPIRIT POWER

God wants us to be filled with the holy presence of His Spirit when we sing and minister in music. It is not talent that breaks the yoke over people's lives and sets the captive free. It is not your musical ability that brings God's glorious power. It is God's Spirit and His presence that makes the difference in music ministry.

God said through the prophet Zechariah..

> Not by might, nor by power, but by
> my spirit says the Lord of hosts.
>
> Zechariah 4:6

MUSIC & THE ANOINTING

In the Old Testament, when a king or priest was to take office, he was anointed: oil was poured upon his head and he was set apart to God.

Oil in the Bible is a type of the Holy Spirit. Without the presence of the Holy Spirit in our lives and ministry we have nothing to offer except mere melodies and lyrics of men's creation. But when we are anointed, and the presence of the Holy Spirit is upon our instruments and voices, great things happen.

We can't anoint ourselves. It is Jesus who pours the oil of the Holy Spirit on those He chooses. We can desire to be anointed but Jesus ultimately calls, appoints and anoints those of character and passion for Him. He responds to our heart and not our art.

DISCUSSION

14. What does Dr. Hayford's comment about worship music "inviting the dominion of His Kingdom" mean to you?

_____
_____
_____
_____
_____

16. How does what Zechariah 4:6 says apply to music and musicians?

_____
_____
_____
_____
_____

17. What can you do to be chosen by Jesus and be anointed so that the power of God and the presence of His Holy Spirit will rest upon you and your music?

_____
_____
_____
_____
_____

18. C. S. Lewis said, "It is in the process of being worshipped that God communicates His presence to men." What does that mean to you?
_____
_____
_____
_____
_____

19. In summary, what is your take-away of the subject music and God's presence?
_____
_____
_____
_____
_____
_____
_____
_____
_____
_____
_____
_____
_____

5

LESSON FIVE
MUSIC AND THE PROPHETIC

*"You will meet a procession of musicians...
they will be prophesying. The Spirit
of God will come upon you..."*

– Samuel, the Prophet

LESSON FIVE - MUSIC AND THE PROPHETIC
STUDY GUIDE

MUSIC & PROPHECY

Throughout Scriptures there is a strong connection between music and prophecy. For example, songs are included in the canon of Holy Scriptures. There are songs in all major sections of the Bible - The Pentetuch, the Historical books, the Poetic books, the Major Prophets, the Minor Prophets, the Gospels, the book of Acts, the Pauline Epistles, the Apocalypse. Of course, the Word of God is considered the highest level of prophecy.

The second highest level of prophecy is the ministry of the prophet. There are numerous accounts of prophets in the Bible singing their prophesies. They are also examples of music being played as the prophet prophesies.

There are also accounts of the spirit of prophesy coming to a person or group and they begin to prophesy though they are not prophets. Music was present in some of these occassions as well.

The reason for this dynamic connection between music and prophesy is because the Holy Spirit is musical. God loves music and creates music within us by His Holy Spirit. One of the indications of this is when you are filled with the Holy Spirit you sing.

> ...be filled with the Holy Spirit singing
> psalms and hymns and spiritual
> songs among yourselves, and making
> music to the Lord in your hearts.
>
> Ephesians 5:18,19

KINGDOM MUSICIANS

1. All books of the Bible are considered inspired of God. Which two books are considered musical?

_____
_____
_____
_____
_____

2. Who are the authors of the songs of prayer and praise in the book of Psalms?

_____
_____
_____
_____
_____

3. How many songs did David prophesy in the Book of Psalms?

_____

_____

_____

_____

4. Very possibly some of the prophesies in the Bible predicting the events about Jesus were sung. List the scripture reference of three of them.

_____

_____

_____

_____

5. When the Holy Spirit comes upon someone often He expresses Himself in song. Can you give an example?

_____

_____

_____

_____

_____

PROPHETIC MUSICIANS

6. What did King David do to encourage prophesy with musical instruments in 1 Chronicles 25:1?

_____
_____
_____
_____
_____

7. Explain what the musicians did on their instruments in 1 Chronicles 25:3.

_____
_____
_____
_____
_____

8. What instruments did the musicians play in 1 Chronicles 25:1,3,7?

_____
_____
_____
_____
_____
_____

9. How many musicians were appointed to play and sing prophetically by King David in 1 Chronicles 25:7?

_____
_____
_____
_____

10. What did Samuel predict Saul would experience in 1 Samuel 10:5-6?

_____
_____
_____
_____

11. What did Saul experience when he met the musicians in 1 Samuel 10:10?

_____
_____
_____
_____
_____
_____

12. In your opinion what was occurring spiritually when the musicians were playing their instruments and prophesying, and suddenly Saul prophesied with them?

_____
_____
_____
_____
_____

13. Elisha the prophet knew the power and importance of music with prophecy. What did he do when he could not prophecy because of the presence of the evil King of Israel in 2 Kings 3:15?

_____
_____
_____
_____
_____

14. Explain what happened when Elisha called for a musician to come and play and why.

_____
_____
_____
_____
_____

15. Why did the prophets have musical instruments in 1 Samuel 10?

_____
_____
_____
_____

16. Describe an account where you experienced divine inspiration in music?

_____
_____
_____
_____

17. In 1 Corinthians 14:39 we are told to intensely desire something. What is that?

_____
_____
_____
_____
_____
_____
_____

IN ADDITION

PROPHESY IN MUSIC

Paul encourages you to earnestly desire and intensely pursue to prophesy yet few believers do. Even fewer musicians pursue to prophesy. Yet prophetic utterance in song is a key expression of the Holy Spirit. He inspires you with thoughts. Thoughts of goodness. Thoughts that edify and encourage. When you sing or play them by inspiration you are doing so prophetically.

You see prophecy in the Old Testament means to speak or sing by inspiration. That is what happened to Saul in 1 Samuel 10. He heard the band of prophetic musicians playing and singing by inspiration of the Holy Spirit and that same Spirit, or anointing, that was on the prophets came on Saul. It was a supernatural event. The key was the impetus of the Holy Spirit in music that caused that miracle.

PROPHECY MEANS TO SPEAK OR SING BY INSPIRATION

These musical prophets were the first worship team mentioned in the Bible. They were part of a school of prophets that Samuel created to equip young men in hearing God and prophesying. To do that Samuel trained them in the Word of God. They had to learn the first five books of the Old Testament - the Pentateuch. They were to get the Word of God in them because we prophesy according to scripture.

Secondly, they were trained in worship and music. They had to know how to get into the inspired state. God's presence came to them when they worshiped in song and with musical instruments. They learned the role that music plays in prophecy.

That is why when the school of young men were coming down from the place of worship they were singing and playing by inspiration of God. They were prophesying. They changed the atmosphere. Even people around them, who were not prophets, spontaneously spoke by inspiration of the Holy Spirit. Why? Because the presence of the Holy Spirit was there. He inspires us when He is present with us in power.

> **THE HOLY SPIRIT INSPIRES US WHEN HE IS PRESENT WITH US IN POWER**

Thirdly, this school of prophets had to learn to prophesy. They practiced encouraging others with their inspired words and melodies. Perhaps they found it easier to prophesy with melodies and rythmns. You see, when you prophesy you have a choice to speak or sing those inspired words.

Have you ever written a song so quickly it was like it just came to you? That was the Holy Spirit inspiring you-- pushing that song into your spirit and mind. It was like a prophetic download. God is challenging you to passionately desire to prophesy in music more often.

DISCUSSION

18. Who was the first worship team mentioned in the Bible and what is the scripture reference?

_____
_____
_____
_____
_____

19. What were the three things that the school of prophets had to do to be trained and why?

_____
_____
_____
_____
_____

20. What does singing and playing musical instruments have to do with prophesying?

_____
_____
_____
_____
_____
_____

6

LESSON SIX
MUSIC IN WAR

"Lucifer rebelled against God…one third of the angelic hosts of the universe may have joined him in his rebellion. Thus the war that started in heaven continues on earth…"

– Billy Graham

LESSON SIX - MUSIC IN WAR
STUDY GUIDE

There is a battle raging all around you and it cannot be seen because it is the spiritual realm. It is between you and the demons that want to steal, kill and destroy you.

> And the dragon (the serpent of old who is the devil and Satan) was enraged with the woman (Israel), and he went to make war with the rest of her offspring, who keep the commandments of God and have the testimony of Jesus Christ.
>
> Revelation 12:17

MILITARY MUSICIANS

You endeavor to follow the instructions in scripture and testify that Jesus saved you from the penalty of your sins. Correct? If so, then the devil has come to make war with you and your loved ones. He wants to mess you up!

> "Be well balanced (temperate, sober of mind), be vigilant and cautious at all times; for that enemy of yours, the devil, roams around like a lion roaring [in fierce hunger], seeking someone to seize upon and devour."

1 Peter 5:8 (Amp)

GAME OF THRONES

You are not struggling with people in your life. You are struggling with spirit powers--master spirits. There are spiritual armed forces who want the throne of your heart. That is why this is a battle of thrones - kingdom of darkness against the kingdom of light.

> For we are not wrestling with flesh and blood [contending only with physical opponents], but against the despotisms, against the powers, against [the master spirits who are] the world rulers of this present darkness, against the spirit forces of wickedness in the heavenly (supernatural) sphere.
>
> Eph 6:11,12 (Amp)

SOME OF THOSE SUPERNATURAL WEAPONS FOR SPIRITUAL WARFARE ARE MUSICAL

Your enemy is a spiritual enemy. He is angry and hungry looking to find some unsuspecting victim to bite into and eat up. He wants to consume lives of mortals especially if you are a Christian. So you have to fight him in the spiritual dimension with spiritual weapons to drive him away.

God has provided those weapons for you to have victory over Satan. Some of those supernatural weapons for spiritual warfare are musical.

SONGS THAT TAKE PRISONERS

God has commanded His people to...

> Let the high praises of God be in their mouth,
> and a two-edged sword in their hand.
>
> Psalms 149:6

God wants His army not only to be equipped with the sword of the Spirit – God's Word – but also with praise.

HE RULES AND ROCKS THE ATMOSPHERE IN THE PLACE YOU PRAISE

Note: This praise is not ordinary praise but "high praise." It comes out of your mouth with volume and authority.

The praise mentioned in this verse is called "tehillah" in Hebrew. It is the spontaneous praises that exalt God. "Tehillah" is called the new song in Psalms 40:3. It is also the praise God dwells in, or is enthroned in (Psalms 22:3).

When you sing this extemporaneous song God sits as king in your praise. Your songs of "tehillah" forms a throne and He rules and rocks the atmosphere in the place you praise.

What is the church-militant going to do with these swords and high praises? The Bible says they are going...

> To execute vengeance upon the heathen, and
> punishments upon the people; To bind their kings
> (rulers of darkness) with chains, and their nobles

with fetters of iron; To execute upon them the judgment written: this honor have all his saints.

Psalms.149:7-9

When you sing loud spontaneous praise to God you bind or restrict the rulers of darkness. You take prisoner demon kings, and powers of the underworld. You bind and constrain them and their influence in your life.

With these spontaneous new songs you will be able to drive out darkness, fight in the spiritual realm and bind the powers of the darkness which try to force their evil will on you and your family.

1. Describe the times that you have sensed spiritual darkness in a place?

_____
_____
_____
_____

2. What did you do in response to evil darkness?

_____
_____
_____
_____

3. How can high praises make any difference against an invisible and spiritual enemy?

_____
_____
_____
_____
_____

4. What two things does God want us to be equipped and armed with based on Psalms 149?

_____
_____
_____
_____
_____

MUSICAL WAR

5. How were musical instruments used in Joshua 6 to take the city and defeat the enemy?

_____
_____
_____
_____
_____

6. You fight an spiritual enemy with spiritual weapons. What are some of the spiritual weapons you can use?

_____
_____
_____
_____
_____

7. What was Joshua's secret weapon that his military carried around the city?

_____
_____
_____
_____
_____

A SONG OF DELIVERANCE

8. There is another army in 2 Chronicles 20 that experienced victory over armies that outnumbered them. How did they use music to defeat their enemies?

_____
_____
_____
_____
_____

9. What did God do in 2 Chronicles 20 to help the worshipers that were singing?

_____
_____
_____
_____

10. What were the lyrics of the song they sang in 2 Chronicles 20 and how were they significant?

_____
_____
_____
_____

11. How did the presence of God affect the outcome of Jehoshaphat's army of worshipers?

_____
_____
_____
_____
_____
_____

IN ADDITION

FIGHT WITH SONG

Jehoshaphat was a worshipper who had a deep reverence for God. After the enemy was seriously defeated with only the "high praises" weapon because of their deep gratitude all the men went to the house of God with their musical instruments and thanked and praised God for the victory.

> Then all the men returned to Jerusalem, with Jehoshaphat leading them, overjoyed that the Lord had given them victory over their enemies..,They marched into Jerusalem to the music of harps, lyres, and trumpets, and they proceeded to the Temple of the Lord.
>
> 2 Chronicles 20:24-28 (NLT)

ROCKETS AND WARHEADS

THE WARHEAD IS THE POWER OF THE HOLY SPIRIT IN OUR MUSIC.

It is important to understand the difference between our weapons and the real power. Just like in an ICBM (intercontinental ballistic missile) the rocket is not where the power is. The rocket is simply the vehicle of transport for the warhead, which has the power of destruction.

Our music making and even our high praises do not have power to destroy the enemy. Rather it is the warhead of God's manifest presence that makes the difference.

The scripture says, "He dwells in the (singing) praises of His people" (Ps 22:3). God makes the difference. He fights for us. Jesus' manifest presence in our musical praise is what defeats the enemy, heals the sick and raises the dead.

Our musical art or craft, used to praise, is only the rocket. The warhead is the power of the Holy Spirit in our music. That is what arms our praise with spiritual power. Always remember it is God that brings us the victory.

DISCUSSION

12. Why is it important to praise God in our spiritual battles?

_____
_____
_____
_____

13. What is the rocket and what is the warhead in our praise and worship?

_____
_____
_____
_____

7

LESSON SEVEN
MUSIC AND HEALING

"My heart, which is so full to overflowing,
has often been solaced and refreshed
by music when sick and weary."
- Martin Luther

LESSON SEVEN - MUSIC AND HEALING

WORK GUIDE

HEALTH AND MUSIC

> Beloved, I pray that you may prosper in every way and [that your body] may keep well, even as [I know] your soul keeps well and prospers.
>
> 3 John 1:2 (Amp)

Did you know that the natural sounds of music can heal? People can find relief from nerve tension and fatigued minds can be restored with music. Music can bring joy and peace to a heart that is upset and troubled. Music can even reverse sickness and bring healing. Yes, music, in the natural, can be used in a positive way to restore a person both physically and mentally. If it can restore physical health, think of what it can do to restore your spiritual health.

MUSIC CAN REVERSE SICKNESS AND BRING HEALING.

MUSIC THERAPY

Beverly Merz, Executive Editor, Harvard "Women's Health Watch" said, "Listening to music reduces anxiety and quells nausea and vomiting associated with chemotherapy and radiotherapy."

"In a hospital intensive-care unit, patients on ventilators who listen to music of their choice actually relax, while those who don't hear music grow more tense. Exciting research suggests that the brain responds to music almost as if it were medicine."

"In a world where vibration reigns supreme, the sounds and vibrations that fill the world outside of us can influence and change the vibrations inside of us, affecting our health and well being for better or for worse. The converse would also be true—the vibrations emanating from inside of us affect and change what takes place in the environment outside of us."

MUSIC PERSCRIPTIONS

Treat your own sickness with the music that will best help you. Here are some guidelines in using the music you like best to deal with your health problems.

Depressed? See a doctor. But if you are just in a prolonged blue mood try playing some of your favorite upbeat, energetic, rhythmical songs. Try moving to the music and let it move you.

Need to get some sleep? University of Louisville School of Nursing discovered in a study that Classical and New Age music helped twenty-four out of twenty-five people with sleeping problems nod off more quickly, sleep for greater periods of time, and get back to sleep more easily after awakening in the middle of the night.

If you have the same problem try quiet, melodic pieces with a slow beat and few rhythmic accents. Classical music of all periods works well and peaceful worship music that invokes the presence of God is even better.

A listening strategy might be start to gear down after supper, skip coffee, and avoid telephone calls and TV after 9 PM. Play softer and quieter music as bedtime approaches. Let your spirit commune with the Lord and heaven's realm of angels and cherubs. Continue listening in bed and set the music to go off a few minutes later.

If stressed out try listening to soothing melodies that can ease anxious feeling and quiet both blood pressure and heart rate. "Everyday stress responds to music too," says Dr. Hanser, who leads a weekly music-therapy, stress-reduction program at Berklee College of Music.

She recommends finding music that will get your attention and at the same time relax your body. Listen to this music in a comfortable position (either lying or sitting down) in a place you will not be disturbed. Focus on the music and after a couple minutes tighten and then relax your muscles. After about ten minutes you can feel refreshed. Afterwards, you may be able to think more clearly and feel more positive and relaxed.

Music's natural qualties can heal, rejuvenate and relax its listener. It can even send vibrations that affect parts of our body.

HEALING FREQUENCIES

Modern science has begun to recognize that the ancient mystics knew for millenniums everything is in a state of vibration. Sound is produced when something vibrates. As most molecular structure move or vibrate they produce sound.

Everything has an optimum range of vibration (frequency) and that range is called resonance. Every organ and cell in our bodies absorbs and emits sound with a particular optimum resonate frequency. When we are in 528 resonance we are in balance.

528 HZ IS THE FREQUENCY USED TO HEAL

Listening to frequencies inside of the optimum range resonate frequency helps our bodies. For example 528 Hz is said to be the "love frequency." 528Hz is also the "miracle" note of the original Solfeggio musical scale. Independently confirmed by researchers 528Hz is the frequency used to heal.

Compared to standard A 440Hz tuning, 528Hz is 4Hz above standard tuning; A 444Hz. When music is tuned to A444Hz it resonates with middle C as 528Hz. 528Hz is the bioenergy of health and longevity. Some researchers say it is the harmonic vibration that lifts your heart.

The frequency 528Hz resonates at the center of the sun (recorded by NASA scientists). Sunbeams, the rainbow, flowers, grass and even the buzzing of bees vibrate at

528Hz. Nature in balance vibrates at this rate. It is the frequency of life itself.

Chlorophyll, and its green and yellow color, vibrates at 528Hz, and is the most powerful healing pigment in biology. It is why people and animals eat grass to regain health.

SUPERNATURAL HEALING

Those are positive natural affects of music. Music can be used spiritually, as well, to facilitate healing. The Biblical principle of music making can heal spiritually. Musicians, and those who are sick, take note. Here is a tool that can help you tremendously. Certain music used a certain way has the power and ability to set your mind and spirit free.

1. Does God desire that we be healthy and if so why?

_____
_____
_____
_____
_____

2. Name three ways that music heals.

_____
_____
_____
_____
_____

MUSIC MEDICINE

3. How can amnesia be treated with music?

_____
_____
_____
_____
_____

4. Sociologists say that music can communicate, influence and then control our spirit, mind and body. How do you suppose music can do that?

_____
_____
_____
_____
_____

MOZART AND MIRACLES

5. There have been historical accounts of healing with music in many cultures. List two and what happened.

_____
_____
_____
_____

6. In the textbook Dr. Gaynor states the first evidences that music has healing potential. Name two of them.

___

MUSICIAN IN THE HOUSE?

7. There was a time when King Saul was depressed and had very bad headaches. In 1 Samuel 16 what did Saul's servants suggest might heal him?

___

8. What was Saul's response?

___

9. What qualification did King Saul request of the musician in 1 Samuel 16:17?

_____
_____
_____
_____
_____

10. Who was the musician mentioned in 1 Samuel 16 and what were his qualities?

_____
_____
_____
_____
_____

11. In your opinion what was special about David and his music that brought supernatural results?

_____
_____
_____
_____
_____
_____
_____

MUSIC MALADY

12. Music can heal but it also can make a person sick. How does music cause pain and discomfort?

_____
_____
_____
_____
_____

13. How can sound waves kill?

_____
_____
_____
_____
_____
_____
_____
_____
_____
_____
_____
_____
_____

IN ADDITION

THE HEALER

Healing is so much a part of God's nature of goodness and kindness that it is one of His names - Jehovah Rapha.

> For I am the Lord who heals you.
>
> Exodus 15:26

Just as Jesus is the One, "Who forgives all your iniquities," (Ps 103:3a) so He is the One "Who heals all your diseases," (Ps 103:3b). David declared salvation and healing go together. He also says, your youth will be renewed. (Ps 103:5) Do you feel older and weaker? Declare God's desire to renew your youth.

Paul declared,

> …God anointed Jesus of Nazareth with the
> Holy Spirit and with power, who went about
> doing good and healing all who were oppressed
> by the devil, for God was with Him.
>
> Acts 10:38

The prophet Malachi spoke by inspiration of the Holy Spirit and said,

> The Sun of Righteousness shall arise
> with healing in His wings.
>
> Malachi 4:2

Your loving Father not only heals physically but also heals hearts that are broken and binds up our emotional wounds. (Ps 147:3) He heals through our faith and our prayers but He also heals us by His presence in our music when we worship Him.

WORSHIP HEALS

Did you know it is possible when we "kiss the Son" in worship we can receive healing? When God inhabits our praises with His revealed essence His healing nature is present. He is the Lord that heals. Not "that" healed once in the past but the God that heals now and continues to heal.

Tom Davis, with AmberRose Ministries, tells of those who were healed by playing a CD of worship music and the word of God in the room with the sick. He reports of cancer disappearing, a deformed baby born normal and a person healed of Leukemia all because worship music and the reading of God's Word was played. Tom has seen miraculous things happen in the lives of the sick and dying from the CD.

Maurice Sklar says that when he plays his violin in worship to God people are often healed. He said, "I have seen nearly every miracle that took place in the gospels with my own eyes. I have seen the lame walk, the deaf hear. I have watched God open the eyes of the blind. I have seen cancer healed. I have seen growths and tumors instantly disappear."

He testifies, "I have noticed that nearly every time miracles like this have occurred, music and worship have been directly connected with them."

DISCUSSION

14. According to Exodus 15, why is it God's nature to heal?

_____
_____
_____
_____

15. David connected salvation and healing in the song he sang in Psalms 103. What does that song say to you?

_____
_____
_____
_____

16. How is musical praise and worship connected with healing

_____
_____
_____
_____

8

LESSON EIGHT
MUSIC AND EXORCISM

"Many evil spirits were cast out, screaming as they left their victims."

- Luke, the Physician

LESSON EIGHT - MUSIC AND EXORCISM
STUDY GUIDE

WE HAVE COMPANY

She walked into the church with such confidence and poise. Her hair was elegantly pinned up and her high-heeled boots were topped with fur as she floated to the front of the sanctuary.

"Wow! Who is she?" We thought to ourselves.

"Obviously someone of importance!"

> I COULD FEEL THE TEARS GATHERING BEHIND MY EYES

She glided gracefully down the aisle while the fox head on her fur shawl stared at us. Her hands were hidden in black gloves and her jewels sparkled. It was one of the more unusual outfits I've seen a woman wear to a worship service. But we were in Athens, Greece. "Maybe they dress differently here." I thought to myself.

The worship that morning was exceptional. The people were passionate for God so it was easy to lead them into His presence. We sang several worship songs and then we we let everyone sing their own personal song. All of the sudden there was sense of power in the room. It was overwhelming.

I knelt to the ground and bowed my head over my guitar. We were in the presence of the Holy presence of God. I could feel the tears gathering behind my eyes. The people were loudly singing their songs of praise to God. The team of musicians with me stopped playing their instruments. The people had control of the service now. God was in the midst of us in power. I glanced over at the keyboardist who was kneeling beside his keyboard. The bass guitar player was laying over his guitar and the drummer knelt at his drum stool with his hands in the air. We were broken in the manifest presence and power of the Almighty.

> **GOD HAD EXPOSED THE DEMON IN THIS WOMAN AND IT WAS FIGHTING TO KEEP ITS HIDING PLACE**

The praise was loud and sounded like "many waters.' In the midst of the roar, I heard screams. I glanced down to the front row to see what the commotion was. The fox lady was writhing on the floor causing her hair to fall into her face. She was not acting like a lady now. She was acting out of character and thrashing about like a wild animal.

I said to myself, "We have company!"

Not only was there a sweet and strong presence of God in the room but there was the presence of evil spirits as well. The power of God had exposed the demon in this woman and it was fighting to keep its hiding place. The revealed presence of God exposed it.

The demon resisted for awhile and then came out and left the woman. She was finally free from power that had found an opening into her life and crawled in. The presence of God in worship had released her from her tormentor.

The powerful thing was God's manifest presence in musical praise and worship had exposed and expelled the evil spirit. The woman was free, smiling and laughing.

EXORCISM WITH A GUITAR

1. When King Saul was manifesting the presence of an evil spirit what did David do when asked to help him in 1 Samuel 16:23?

_____
_____
_____
_____

2. Besides David's character, courage, and conduct, what was the most notable thing about David? (1 Samuel 16:18b)

_____
_____
_____
_____
_____

3. According to the author, what is the key to signs and wonders in musical praise?

_____
_____
_____
_____
_____

4. What kind of music do you think David played when the evil spirit left Saul--testimonial songs, popular songs, liturgical songs, worship songs?

_____
_____
_____
_____
_____

5. Describe the instrument that David played for Saul.

_____
_____
_____
_____
_____
_____
_____

MUSICIANS EXPEL DEMONS

6. Describe a time when you experienced the presence of evil. If you expelled the demon, how did you do it?

___
___
___
___
___
___
___
___
___
___
___
___
___
___
___
___
___
___
___
___
___

7. When you experienced the presence of evil spirits, what did you do about it?

IN ADDITION

SONGS THAT TAKE PRISONERS

God has commanded His people to...

> Let the high praises of God be in their mouth,
> and a two-edged sword in their hand
>
> Psalms 149:6

God wants His army not only to be equipped with the sword of the Spirit – God's Word – but also with praise. Note, this praise is not ordinary praise but "high praise." This is praise that comes out of your mouth with volume and authority.

When you sing this extemporaneous song God sits as king in your praise. Your songs of "tehillah" form a throne for God to sit. Not that He needs one. He has one but the power and authority of His throne is revealed. God rules and rocks the atmosphere in that place where you praise.

What are you and I going to do with these swords and high praises? The Bible says they are going...

> To execute vengeance upon the heathen,
> and punishments upon the people; To

> bind their kings (rulers of darkness) with chains, and their nobles with fetters of iron; To execute upon them the judgment written: this honor have all his saints.
>
> Psalms 149:7-9 (KJV emphasis mine)

This scripture says when you sing loud spontaneous songs in praise to God you spiritually tie up rulers of darkness. You take demon kings and powers of the underworld prisoner. You bind and restrict their influence in your life.

If you are presently in a spiritual struggle be encouraged. Jesus said to His followers…

> I saw Satan fall like lightning from heaven. Behold I give you authority to trample on serpents and scorpions, and over all the power of the enemy, and nothing shall by any means hurt you…
>
> Luke 10:18,19

The word serpents and scorpions are not literal snakes and bugs. They are metaphors for evil and unclean spirits.

What the scripture is saying is that you have been given authority to put demons and evil spirits under your feet. So sing the high praise to God and let His presence and power expose and expel the presence of evil in your life.

DISCUSSION

13. Describe the 'high praises' mentioned in Psalms 149.

_____
_____
_____
_____
_____

14. What effect does 'high praise' have on dark powers according to Psalms 149?

_____
_____
_____
_____
_____

15. What was Jesus saying in Luke 10 to encourage His disciples? How does that encourage you?

_____
_____
_____
_____
_____
_____
_____

9

LESSON NINE
WHICH MUSIC IS OKAY?

"All music takes you somewhere, you just need to find out where the music your listening to is taking you"

- Unknown

LESSON NINE - WHICH MUSIC IS OKAY?
STUDY GUIDE

GOD'S MUSIC

For thousands of years God has been praised with music by Christians around the world. Some have used such primitive instruments as a nose flute or a single stringed instrument made from sheep instestine and still others with the massive sound of a pipe organ.

DRUMS ARE TOO VULGAR FOR THE WORSHIP OF GOD

Some churches and movements believe that only melody is acceptable to God in worship while others believe that only German should be sung in worship-- other languages were too secular. Some Christian denominations teach that drums or any type of rhythm is too vulagar for the worship of God. While others teach that instruments should not be used in the sanctuary to worship God.

Why is there so much controversy about music in worship among Christians? Why are not all Christian denominations and movements on the same page? Why don't we know the truth about which music, musical instruments or styles of music are acceptable to God and to be used in the worship of Him? I'll tell you the answer. Few leaders have a theology of music. Not many leaders know what the Bible says about music. That is why this study is so important. We all must know the role and purpose of music in the kingdom of God.

WHICH MUSICAL INSTRUMENTS?

1. In some Christian movements there is controversy over which instruments you can use in worship of God. In some cases, no instruments can be used to worship God in the sanctuary. According to Psalms 81:1-3, what category of instruments are we supposed to play in worship to God?

_____
_____
_____
_____
_____

2. What other instruments are we to use in praise to God mentioned in Psalm 150:3-5?

_____
_____
_____
_____
_____

3. What musical instruments does 2 Samuel 6:5 tell us to use in worshiping God?

_____
_____
_____
_____
_____

4. In 1 Chronicles 16:42 what do you think the term "musical instruments of God" means?

_____
_____
_____
_____
_____

5. What instruments are we commanded to praise God with in Psalms 81:1-3 and Psalms 150:3-5?

_____
_____
_____
_____
_____
_____
_____

WHICH MUSIC IS OKAY?

6. Where did music come from originally?

_____
_____
_____
_____

7. What is the danger of your music being too close to the world and its spirit?

_____
_____
_____
_____

8. According to James 4:4, what happens if we, or our music making, are too world-friendly?

_____
_____
_____
_____
_____

SONGS OF THE WORLD

9. What is the difference between "songs of the Lord" and "songs of the world?"

_____
_____
_____
_____
_____
_____
_____

10. Describe the difference between "songs of the world," "songs of the flesh," and "songs of the devil."

_____
_____
_____
_____
_____

11. What negative affect has "music of the flesh" and "music of the devil" on a person?

_____
_____
_____
_____
_____

SONGS OF THE LORD

12. What does Philippians 4:8 say that points to what songs are the best for us to listen to?

_____
_____
_____
_____

13. Describe the type of songs that God recommends and that edify us.

_____
_____
_____
_____

THE POWER OF MUSIC

14. Describe how music is both powerful and influential.

_____
_____
_____
_____

LOVE NOT THE WORLD--AND ITS MUSIC

15. 1 John 2:15 says, "Do not love the world or the things in the world. If anyone loves the world, the love of the Father is not in him." (ESV). What does that tell us about the music of the world?

_____
_____
_____
_____

LOVE NOT THE WORLD--AND ITS MUSIC

16. There are three ways to determine if a song has healthy content or not. One is the lyric. What should you look for in the lyrics to see if it is good for the listener?

_____
_____
_____
_____
_____
_____

17. What is the second way to judge a song and what should you look for?

_____
_____
_____
_____

18. What is the third way to judge a song and what would you look for?

_____
_____
_____
_____

HOW DOES GOD LIKE HIS MUSIC?

19. In 2 Chronicles 30:21, how was music played to God?

_____
_____
_____
_____
_____

20. 1 Chronicles 16:25 says how we are to praise the Lord. The same instruction occurs four times in the Bible. What does that say to you about how you should praise the Lord?

_____
_____
_____
_____
_____

21. Besides lifting up the voice and playing musical instruments with fortissimo, what other ways does Ephesians 5:19 say God likes music?

_____
_____
_____
_____
_____

IN ADDITION

MUSIC OF THE KINGDOM OF GOD

Reading and studying the one thousand plus mentions of music in the Bible gives you an idea of what music in God's kingdom is like. Keep in mind the music of the kingdom may not be the same as music of the church or even pop culture worship music.

The kingdom of God is the realm and domain over which God rules. When men's opinions and preferences circumvent God's will or desire then that entity is no longer part of the domain of God. It is not under the rule or authority of God.

Music in our culture is so personal because of it accessibility that most Christians don't discern what music is good for them and which is not. Music is everywhere and always available so you might not make a moral judgement on what you are listening to.

Music of the darkness of this world is under the domain of Satan. His music kills life and goodness. It destroys morals and people. It is poison and shouldn't be ingested. Just as when you are suspicious something in your drink or food might not be good for you, so likewise be suspicious of what is in the music you injest.

I am convinced in studying the music of the Bible that besides people, one of God's favorite things is the songs His people sing to Him. Enjoy God! Enjoy good healthy music!

DISCUSSION

22. How is music in God's kingdom different than the music that is elsewhere?

_____
_____
_____
_____
_____
_____
_____
_____
_____

23. What did the Holy Spirit speak to you about in this chapter?

_____
_____
_____
_____
_____
_____
_____
_____
_____

10

LESSON TEN
MUSIC, RESTORATION, AND REVIVAL

"You show me a church that loves to sing to God and I'll show you a church that is spiritually alive."

- LaMar Boschman

LESSON TEN - MUSIC, RESTORATION, & REVIVAL
WORK GUIDE

REVIVED MUSIC

Throughout Biblical history and church history music has been a result of renewal and revival. From each spiritual awakening has come a new expression in song. The restoration of worship under David, Hezekiah and Nehemiah music was restored along with the spiritual renewal.

Then in church history from the Upper Room and worship of the Early Church to the Reformation, Azusa Street revival, and Charismatic movement, new songs of faith and revival were birthed. Singing of praise and worship was a vital part of the Latter Rain, Jesus People, and Charismatic movements as well as the Toronto Blessing and Brownsville revival.

Singing praise and worship to God has always been a sign of spiritual awakening. It is a key to being revived and alive to God. Passionate musical expressions to God are a sign of a fervent spiritual heart.

1. Music was a key part of King David's worship of God. What elaborate arrangements did he make, in 1 Chronicles 25, to use music to worship God?

_____
_____
_____
_____
_____

2. Explain what restoration and revival mean.

_____
_____
_____
_____
_____

REVIVAL MUSIC

3. With most revivals and renewals of the Holy Spirit there has been a renewal of music. New music is a result of spiritual renewal. Why is this so?

_____
_____
_____
_____
_____

4. During a dark period of church history, only the clergy could sing in public worship of God in perscribed chants and prayers. For almost one thousand years, believers were not allowed to sing in the church. What changed that?

_____
_____
_____
_____

5. With the numerous renewals in the 1900's music had a role in each. Describe three of those renewals and how music was part of each.

_____
_____
_____
_____
_____
_____
_____
_____
_____
_____
_____

6. Describe what "psalms" means in the Hebrew in the Old Testament and Greek in the New Testament.

_____
_____
_____
_____
_____

7. Describe the definition of hymns in the New Testament.

_____
_____
_____
_____
_____

8. In the 1970's and 1980's there was a renewal in "spiritual songs." What does spiritual songs mean in Ephesians 5:19?

_____
_____
_____
_____
_____
_____
_____
_____

ANCIENT WORSHIP REFORMATIONS

9. What happened musically in the revival in Nehemiah 7?

10. In 2 Chronicles 23:18 there is another renewal of worship. What did the priest Jehoiada do with the musicians?

11. When Israel fell into idolatry (putting other things before God), what was one of the first things to deteriorate?

12. Describe the music mentioned in Exodus 32 that backslidden Israel used in their idol worship.

_____
_____
_____
_____

13. What does the decay of Israel's relationship with God and the change in their music say to you?

_____
_____
_____
_____

MUSIC IS IMPORTANT TO GOD

14. Under the great renewal of Hezekiah mentioned in 2 Chronicles 29:25-28, what happened musically with musicians, singers and musical instrument?

_____
_____
_____
_____
_____

IN ADDITION

RENEWAL AND NEW SONGS

With most every revival in Biblical history and Church history, there was a revival in song. Usually, the song was spontaneous because it was inspired. People were moved spiritually and they began to sing out extemporaneously.

The opposite is true when movements become rigid and somewhat lifeless. The instantaneous songs are not heard anymore in public services. Music becomes rigid and formal and spontaneity is discouraged.

From the reformers in Europe to the Huguenots in Southern France, from the spiritualists in Azusa, CA to the seekers in Toronto, all were inspired by the Holy Spirit and experienced a new expression of singing.

From the Scripture in Song singers in New Zealand to the Charismatic renewal in the US to the worship reformation of the 1980's, music played a huge part in the spiritual rebirth of people and movements.

From the meetings Jesus held to the praises of the newly-birth Church, to the outpouring of the Holy Spirit in the Upper Room, new songs sprang up expressing the spiritual revelation received by those present.

From the Moravians in 1727 to revival meetings of Katherine Kuhlman and Carlos Anacondia, the presence of God that came upon the people, as they sang spontaneously, created an atmosphere for the mighty hand of God to move in signs and wonders.

THE HOLY SPIRIT SINGS

"The baptism in the Holy Spirit upon the Moravians and then the Methodists produced a flood of sacred songs," someone once said of the Moravian revival. Such is true with most outpourings of the Holy Spirit.

This is often the case when the Spirit of God moves in power in a person or movement--inspired song comes forth. This is a fundamental reason why singing is a part of so many renewals, awakenings, and revivals. When the Spirit of the Lord comes to exalt Jesus and show His power, people break forth in song.

This is why Paul says in Ephesians 5 "be filled with the Spirit and sing Spirit songs." The singing of praise to God is a direct effect of the Holy Spirit moving in a person's life. The Holy Spirit sings. He will sing through you when you are filled with Him. There is a spiritual connection between singing and the Holy Spirit.

From the Wailing Wall to a cathedral hall, from shepherd fields to a harvest yield, from Prayer Mountain to the Bethesda fountain songs are a result of the Holy Spirit's blessing and moving among God's people.

The same is true at the birth of Jesus. Song erupted in a mother's womb and in a dark shepherd's field. Singing is what happens when God moves.

DISCUSSION

15. What happens musically when movements are in decline?

_____
_____
_____
_____

16. What is the connection with the Holy Spirit and song? Give examples.

_____
_____
_____
_____
_____
_____
_____
_____
_____
_____
_____
_____

11

LESSON ELEVEN
MUSIC IN HEAVEN

"Praise is the rehearsal of our eternal song. By grace we learn to sing, and in glory we continue to sing."

– Charles Spurgeon

LESSON ELEVEN - MUSIC IN HEAVEN
STUDY GUIDE

THE POPULAR LYRIC

As John peers into heaven through an open door, he sees the reverent and profound worship of the inhabitants there, and he hears the sound of worship on the other side.

THE FIRST SONG OF SOME TWENTY-EIGHT SONGS OF HEAVEN LISTED IN THE APOCALYPSE

> Holy, holy, holy Lord God Almighty, Who was and is and is to come!
>
> Revelation 4:8b

This is the first song of some twenty-eight songs from heaven listed in the Apocalypse. The lyrics the aliens (like nothing seen on earth) sing are about Yahweh and His ominous nature.

It starts with a three-fold affirmation, "Holy, holy, holy," which speaks of the Trinity of the persons of the Godhead, equally divine in their attributes.

Holy is the Father, holy is the Son and holy is the Holy Spirit, three in one. He is holy "who was" and "who is" and "who is to come." The creatures are so captured by who

God is that they never stop, or grow tired of saying this one word, "holy."

Heaven's creatures endlessly declare His greatness, His grandeur, His mystery and His majesty—for He is all that and much more—so why shouldn't we endlessly sing His praises? Why would we stop worshiping Him? Is it possible to come to an end of the acclamations, declarations and proclamations of who He is? Do we run out of descriptions of God who is matchless, peerless and endless in His essence?

God is eternal, continuous, all encompassing, the same yesterday, today and forever, so why would we ever cease to praise Him? He is deserving of continual worship.

Holiness is the quality most basic to the essential nature of God. Scholars say it's His crowning attribute. His holiness sums up all His other attributes—His infinitude, His immutableness, His omniscience, His omnipresence and the rest.

The root word of "holy" means "separate" or "apart," indicating God's self-existence and independence from everything He created. He doesn't need us, or anything from us.

The worship of heaven that comes from these extra-celestials, begins with their acknowledgement of God's holiness. Their transcendent lyrics of the attributes and nature of God are simple, but staggering.

The initial song here in the Apocalypse declares God's design for all of His creatures from the four corners of the earth: All living creatures are to lift up His crowning attribute—His holiness.

1. How many songs are mentioned in the book of Revelation?

_____
_____
_____
_____

2. Why is the word "holy" sung so often and repeatedly in songs of heaven?

_____
_____
_____
_____
_____

THE SINGERS

3. Describe the singers John heard in Revelation 7:9-10.

_____
_____
_____
_____

4, In Revelation 7, what did these worshipers do on earth to end up in heaven?

THE PLAYERS

5. In Revelation 15:2,3, who are the worshipers John describes and what are they singing?

6. Describe the musical instruments the worshipers are playing in Revelation 15:2.

MORE MUSICIANS IN HEAVEN

7. Who are the musicians in Revelation 14:3 and what are they playing?

_____
_____
_____
_____
_____

8. What kind of song are the worshipers in Revelation 14:3 singing?

_____
_____
_____
_____
_____

9. According to the author, why should those who sing and play instruments be encouraged?

_____
_____
_____
_____
_____

10. From all the previous scriptures, describe all those who are playing instruments in heaven.

_____
_____
_____
_____
_____

CHOIR AND ORCHESTRA

11. Describe the worshipers in Revelation 5:13 and who you think they are?

_____
_____
_____
_____
_____

MUSIC MINISTERS WANTED

12. We discovered that the anointed cherub Lucifer was removed from his position worship facilitator in heaven. In your opinion, who will be filling that vacancy if anyone?

_____
_____
_____
_____

13. Why should those that have a gift to play or sing music study music in the Bible?

_____
_____
_____
_____

14. Describe the importance of the ministry of music in heaven?

_____
_____
_____
_____

IN ADDITION

SONGS FROM THE OTHER SIDE

When I consider the music of heaven there are four things that strike me. The numerous sources of song, the volume of their songs, the lyrics of their songs, and the kind of songs they sing.

The source of the songs of heaven are from almost every possible inhabitant. Songs of praise come from angels, elders, overcomers, alien creatures, and every creature in soil, sea and sky. They are all singing the attributes and nature of God.

The voluminous heavenly crescendo is abosolutely defeaning to the mortal ear. It is as the roar of a thousandsoceans. It is compared by Jesus cousin, John, who heard it as extremely loud thunder rattling the air and land.

SPONTANEOUS

The other unique quality about the music of heaven is that most of the singing is extemporaneous. In other words, it is in the moment. As the occupants of heaven behold the radiant attributes of their glorious King they reflect them back in songs and shouts.

There are no artful renderings of previously rehearsed musical arrangments. Interestingly what is missing is the art of music created by man. The music of celestial realm is instantaneous as well as glorious.

There are possibly a few structured songs. John calls them "The Song of Moses" and "The Song of the Lamb." Some scholars consider these songs the title of a single song. The song is called "The Song of Moses and the Song of the Lamb" combining perfectly the old and new covenant. The song is the union of law and love. It encapsulates the first song in the Pentatuch with the last song in Apocalypse. The title of this song mentions the first and last songs in the Bible. This is the alpha and omega song.

DISCUSSION

15. In your opinion, what is unique about the songs of heaven?

_____
_____
_____
_____

16. Why do you think most of the songs in heaven are spontaneous?

_____
_____
_____
_____

17. What will you do or believe differently as a result of studying the music of heaven?

_____
_____
_____
_____
_____

12

LESSON TWELVE
MUSIC AND PRAISE

"God delights in the singing of
His people so much He chose their
spontaneous songs as His habitation"

– LaMar Boschman

LESSON TWELVE - MUSIC AND PRAISE
WORK GUIDE

TERRESTIAL AND CELESTIAL

Praise in scripture is expressed with shouts, prayers, proclamations, clapping, raised hands, testimonies, and so much more. The most common and highest mood of praise is when it is expressed in song.

PRAISE IN SONG OCCURS INSTINCTIVELY WITH MEN AND ANGELS

Praise in song occurs instinctively with men and angels - both terrestials and celestials. It is a natural response to the awareness of the greatness and goodness of God.

> Suddenly, the angel was joined by a vast host of others—the armies of heaven—praising God and saying (with these lyrics) Glory to God in highest heaven, and peace on earth to those with whom God is pleased.
>
> Luke 2:13-14 (NLT)

All of creation - plant, mineral and animal - will all naturally break out in song to their Creator.

> Everything on earth will worship you;
> they will sing your praises, shouting
> your name in glorious songs.
>
> Psalms 66:4 NLT

Praise is best expressed in the tones and the pulse of melody. It is elegant, emotional and deserving to such a wonderful and glorious God.

1. What is the one of the highest expressions of praise?

___
___
___
___
___

2. Is it scriptural that plants and animals sing praises to God? How is that possible?

___
___
___
___
___
___
___
___

ZAMAR WITH A GUITAR

3. Describe the meaning of the Hebrew word "zamar."

___

4. In Psalms 69:30, what pleases God more than the sacrifice of animals of the Old Testament?

___

TEHILLAH - WHERE GOD DWELLS

5. What is the definition of the Hebrew word "tehillah?"

___

MUSIC AND PRAISE 135

6. Write out the scripture with its reference that tells you "tehillah" is a new song.

_____
_____
_____
_____

7. In Psalm 22:3, what is the meaning of the Hebrew word for "praise"?

_____
_____
_____
_____

8. What does the word "enthroned" mean in Psalm 22:3?

_____
_____
_____
_____

9. Explain why "tehillah" music is power music.

_____
_____
_____

10. According to Psalms 100:4 and Isaiah 60:18, why is "tehillah" praise so special?

_____
_____
_____
_____
_____

THE GENESIS OF MUSIC

11. Music was created by God and given to angels first to praise Him. Praise and worship was the original intention and purpose of music. In Colossians 1:16, for who were all things created and why?

_____
_____
_____
_____
_____

12. Write out Revelation 4:11.

_____
_____
_____
_____
_____

13. Why is a new song mentioned in scripture and never an old song?

_____
_____
_____
_____
_____

14. We are instructed to sing praise to God over 280 times in scripture. What does that mean to you?

_____
_____
_____
_____
_____

IN ADDITION

POWER MUSIC

The most significant scripture that contains the Hebrew word "tehillah" is Psalms 22:3." Yet you are holy, enthroned on the praises of Israel."

The phrase "sits enthroned" speaks of royal authority. The praises of God's people are the throne on which the great King sits.

God used to dwell between the cherubim and above the mercy seat on the Ark of the Covenant on which rested the Shekinah-glory. Today God's revealed presence dwells on the tehillah praise of His people.

This throne is a symbol of royal government, supreme power and dignity. It speaks of kingdom authority, kingdom power and the king's role as judge.

The term "sits on the throne" implies the exercise of regal power. When we praise God and He sits on the throne of our praise, there is an exercise of regal power—the result is signs and wonders.

God sits on the throne of His power in the third heaven and also sits on the throne of our praise. In Psalms 22:3 the word "praises" is translated from the Hebrew word "tehillah." It means a song or hymn of praise, adoration or thanksgiving paid to God.

> Praise [tehillah] is awaiting
> You, O God, in Zion…
>
> Psalms 65:1a

Throughout scripture, we see that God is inseparably joined to "tehillah" praise. Where "tehillah" praise is God is. Where God is "tehillah" praise is! This throne of "tehillah" praise is the "throne zone" and the "power zone." Here is where God sits in regal power exercising His complete authority.

15. Describe when you have experienced or seen God's power and presence during spontaneous praise.

_____
_____
_____
_____
_____
_____
_____
_____

16. List a scripture reference for each of the following things that happened in the presence of God: sick are healed, demon exorcised, and people could not stand up.

_____
_____
_____
_____

> "After all, the gift of language combined
> with the gift of song was only given to
> man to let him know that he should praise
> God with both word and music"
>
> - Martin Luther

ABOUT THE AUTHOR
LAMAR BOSCHMAN

A sought after speaker and mentor, LaMar Boschman is a pioneer and a father of contemporary Christian worship. He is known for equipping others in transcendent worship. Here is a snapshot of LaMar in his own words:

From the day my father bought me my first guitar at fourteen years old, I remember the joy I experienced in writing and singing songs. At sixteen, two friends and I recorded our first album and began to pursue singing wherever we were invited, touring around western Canada. After moving to Vancouver, British Columbia, I became part of a musically progressive church and discovered what praise and worship was. Upon finishing Bible college there, God launched me into full-time itinerant ministry—my life would never be the same.

From the age of 22, I became one of the first itinerant worship ministries traveling the world leading worship and teaching about worship and the music of the kingdom of God. Looking back to a time when we only worshiped with piano, organ, and hymn books there were a few of us who created the first worship seminars in the United States. Over the years we have hosted Worship Institutes to equip leaders in many places of the world including Argentina, Belarus, Curacao, Greece, Indonesia, Malaysia, Philippines, Russia, Singapore, Ukraine and the United States.

Today I still teach seminars, speak at conferences, blog, write books, and mentor younger leaders. I live in Roanoke, Texas with my wife and we are members of Gateway Church (www.gatewaypeople.com) where I serve.

WHAT OTHERS SAY

For four decades, LaMar Boschman has helped people connect with the presence of God in spiritual worship and music of the Kingdom. He has been one of the pioneers and fathers of contemporary worship. As the author of numerous books and DVDs, LaMar Boschman's teaching and worship leading has impacted churches and leaders around the world. The gift he carries has changed church cultures and redefined the paths of many church leaders.

"LaMar Boschman's leadership in worship is a continuing gift of the grace of God to the Church today. His timeless promptings to our pursuit of God's praise and glory is worthy of our attention."

— JACK HAYFORD

OTHER RESOURCES

REAL MEN WORSHIP: It isn't easy for most men to be free in their worship of the Lord. Cultural conditioning and long habits have "frozen" them into a sometimes unbiblical and unsatisfying worship experience. Yet, it doesn't have to be that way! Real worship, masculine worship, is full-throated, full-bodied and brimming with energy, passion, and joy. LaMar Boschman helps men find the guts, boldness, and courage to become the passionate worshippers God created them to be.

A HEART OF WORSHIP: Experience a rebirth of worship! This book will energize and invigorate your worship changing the way you view your potential, ability and call to worship. Complete with study guide, *A Heart of Worship* also contains a special section for pastors and worship leaders. Discover your heart of worship.

AVAILABLE AT:
amazon.com and www.LaMarBoschman.com

CONNECT WITH LAMAR

LAMARBOSCHMAN.COM

- Gain fresh revelation on spiritual principles that will empower your music, your worship life and ministry — subscribe to LaMar's blog.

- Discover all of LaMar's books .

- Schedule LaMar to speak at your event.

- Find LaMar's new teaching series on YouTube.

- Follow LaMar on Instagram, Google+, Facebook, and Twitter!

www.ingramcontent.com/pod-product-compliance
Lightning Source LLC
LaVergne TN
LVHW051607070426
835507LV00021B/2821